THE MINDFUL MARRIAGE

THE MINDFUL MARRIAGE

Cultivating a Conscious Relationship

AVERY NIGHTINGALE

QuantumQuill Press

CONTENTS

1　Introduction　　1

2　Understanding Mindful Marriage　　2

3　The Importance of Conscious Relationships　　4

4　Building a Foundation of Trust　　6

5　Effective Communication Techniques　　8

6　Nurturing Emotional Intimacy　　9

7　Enhancing Physical Intimacy　　11

8　Cultivating Mutual Respect　　13

9　Managing Conflict and Resolving Differences　　15

10　Practicing Forgiveness and Letting Go　　17

11　Sustaining Love and Connection　　19

12　Creating Shared Meaning and Purpose　　21

13　Embracing Vulnerability and Authenticity　　23

14　Fostering Emotional Support and Empathy　　25

15　Balancing Independence and Togetherness　　27

16　Cultivating Gratitude and Appreciation　　29

17　Strengthening Friendship and Companionship　　31

Contents

18 Navigating Life Transitions Together   33

19 Mindful Parenting in a Conscious Marriage   34

20 Prioritizing Self-Care and Personal Growth   36

21 Maintaining Work-Life Balance   38

22 Building a Supportive Network   40

23 Exploring Shared Interests and Hobbies   42

24 Cultivating a Sense of Adventure and Fun   44

25 Practicing Mindfulness in Everyday Life   46

26 Deepening Spiritual Connection   48

27 Overcoming Relationship Challenges   50

28 Seeking Professional Help and Guidance   52

29 Fostering Resilience and Adaptability   54

30 Celebrating Milestones and Achievements   56

31 Reflecting on the Journey Together   58

32 Conclusion   60

CHAPTER 1

Introduction

Research in all disciplines on the importance of self-awareness and connection to one's inner life, and of consciously, respectfully connecting with others has exploded in the past twenty-five years. There have been many marriages over the years that have been founded in love, shared values, positive emotions, and a nurturing family environment. A brain-based discipline and the focusing of sophisticated psychodynamics expands and enhances the experience of an established, happy, long-term marriage to a state of continuous discovery and growth. Conveying that belief and its tools to the so-inclined couples becomes the impetus of this book.

Although being married to the same person for 40 or 50 years is less common today, intimate relationships are longer and better than at any prior time. My previous book, Project Renewment: The First Retirement Model for Career Women, was research-based and offered strategies to optimize women's retirement experience. That economic and educational evolution has overflowed gender lines and has created a union in status and roles that enables both genders to make broad contributions to their mutual, individual, and shared professional, societal, and family pursuits. The economic and demographic data suggest that successful marriages have evolved and are more successful than ever.

CHAPTER 2

Understanding Mindful Marriage

The mind and the body conspire to fight against stillness and we feverishly fall into liking, disliking, and ignoring. But every once in a while, almost in spite of ourselves, we connect with the blessed nature of our partner, evoking a kind of love and intimacy that feels pure and rare and fleeting. If change is possible, it can be monumental. Should you desire to improve yourself, make it happen with the satisfying knowledge that it can change the dynamics of an entire union. This feeling may be deep in our beings and intelligent in origin, but its internal forces are so much broader and more mysterious than mere images made by the mind. We don't have to invent sacredness, and we cannot, indeed, because it is always within us. And when we love our partner, or our child, or best friend, we are uncovering a truth of who they really are in much the same way as a physician who saves your life by removing the wood splinters that were drenched in gasoline. You are saved and you are happy for the doctor, but you don't go around declaring your undying devotion to him. The splinters were not him. But now is not about altruism. I confess I'm not totally turned off to the idea of mindfulness and its effect on my marriage because of its potential to change the way my husband experiences me or how I experience him. Mindlessness is like a slumbering python that waits until the second we don't know what to do around each other to snap to and shatter any chance of happiness and compassion. When we are mindful, and words are relevant and kind, we connect to each other in a basic and deep way. His needs then are my needs and my fears are his fears. We are together in a space our two minds have formed, a sanctuary of calm that can do good for us and all we encounter. I won't argue that it will be perfect, and it won't always be easy, but it will be always right to be with him in this way.

To understand marriage and mindfulness, we must first understand both of its parts. A marriage is built on the same principles as Buddhist psychology. A healthy marriage, like the one the Buddha taught, has as its foundation a basic goodness of human nature. Underneath every transgression and neurotic behavior pattern, there is an inherent well-being in people, dormant perhaps, but deeply rooted in awareness. There is within each of us a core which is sacred, resourceful, kind, dignified, and worthy of respect. Imperfection and faults are not the basic truth; rather, they are the temporary obscurations which must be understood and stripped away so that the natural, radiant nature can be discovered. Clearly, this is exactly what happens when we love another human being. First, there is the grace and regality of who the person truly is, a quality we see not through our own idealizing concepts, but through our eyes of wisdom; then, as the living together begins, we lose track of our enlightened view and start reacting to the various nerves and needs we encounter.

CHAPTER 3

The Importance of Conscious Relationships

Self-powered referential relationships look like this: Both individuals have an incredibly clear understanding of the essence, personality, passion, and ultimate desires of the other. Each person is able to manifest their potential and help the other do the same. More concretely, and this part is more challenging - both have learned the act of "re-upping" (a term I coined). When you "re-up", you heighten your arousal, and you make the relationship a priority, reasoning out how to be more loving, more connected.

We often bring to our marriage (or any committed relationship) someone we barely recognize because of familial, societal, and personal factors. We carry outdated and limiting beliefs because of our individual life experiences - often experiencing misunderstanding due to most egoic thoughts and values we hold. To navigate a lifelong partnership with a deeply connected sense of meaning, it's important to cultivate conscious relationships. To limit stress and make significant, mindful shifts in your relationship, you must be committed to your own self-awareness, sharing a flexible life vision you both intend to help shape.

When two people come together in a committed relationship, it's an alchemical process of a union woven beautifully to be more radiant and resilient than would otherwise be possible - full of passion, depth, honesty, and true connection. In these busy, fast-paced times, managing an effortless dance of exclusive partnership is a real challenge. In any committed relationship, there are both day-to-day challenges and complex, subtle aspects of self and systems under the surface.

CHAPTER 4

Building a Foundation of Trust

The consciousness, or mindful aspect, on the other hand, is grounded in actual Being and is limitless. And so it follows that this aspect can be trusted because limitations of the ego don't apply to it. When we manifest Being in relation to another, we are acting as trust would direct. But since ego is corrupt and by its nature seeks other egos to dominate and control, trusting others is itself problematic and risky at best. So, if we should hope to build trust upon a stable and enduring foundation, the answer necessarily begins with the mindful. It describes the extent to which a Being has actualized his or her own potential – the extent to which they have integrated ego with Soul and then defined their love, creativity, discipline, conscience, motive, gratitude, and forgiveness thoughts, words, and actions through it.

Exactly how to create trust in a marriage is perhaps one of the most often recurring questions asked by marriage counselors and relationship experts. From a deeper spiritual perspective, it is trust in the essential and supreme goodness of the human that is the key to love and consciousness in marriage. This is the trust that consciousness, not ego, sustains marriage. Trust is one of the cornerstones upon which we may build an enduring foundation that ensures a relationship is manageable, resilient, and rewarding through the course of time. But where exactly does trust come from and how do we build it in marriage? Consider first that the ego is measurably corrupt and self-centered. It is also a metaphysical liability and, while it can and should be managed and diminished, it cannot be trusted.

CHAPTER 5

Effective Communication Techniques

One way to practice avoiding criticism is to use a practice called the "sandwich method," which encourages you to always say something pleasing before you express a complaint or issue and to follow any criticism up with more pleasing words. Another way to avoid criticism is by acknowledging and taking responsibility for your own triggers. If you are easily triggered by loud noises or feelings of inadequacy, let your partner know that these things are what you believe to be your triggers and ask specifically for help in managing these things. By keeping criticism at bay, all parties can actively listen and respond with understanding and love. This, in turn, helps to keep discussions productive, effective, and empathetic. Recall that a big part of active listening is monitoring and managing our inner critic so that all minds are as present and open as possible to our partner.

Avoiding criticism is an effective way, whether in marriage or any significant relationship. In removing this barrier to real communication, all parties are invited to share in the experience of understanding and connection. In even a caring and truly connected relationship, it is difficult to feel connected to someone who is speaking critically toward you. It is also difficult to stay connected to someone you are speaking critically toward.

CHAPTER 6

Nurturing Emotional Intimacy

Creating an atmosphere focused on emotional intimacy is less about behavior and more about our state of mind. So begins Slowing Down to the Speed of Life, a book about how to reclaim and relish moments of being alive. To live our lives and thrive spiritually, we need to understand the creative power of thought and how it, and our ongoing relationship with it, affect our sense of being and aliveness. Emotional and spiritual intimacy stems from connecting with an aspect of being, then consciously navigating our state of mind experiences involving our relationship to the thoughts, beliefs, and feelings associated with the relationship, which often shape our sense of being. When it comes to relationships with ourselves and others, present state of mind experiences can act as a form of spiritual guidance. Over the years, as difficult as the process may be, gradually changing dysfunctional state of mind experiences within our relationships shapes genuine acceptance of self, others, and relational connections according to support and maintain healthy positive experiences.

The prerequisite for emotional intimacy is the unconditional acceptance of self and partner. Over time, much of the emotional connection between partners becomes an unconscious act that we take for granted until something begins to disrupt that connection. For example, if you fall into the habit of making how much money your spouse earns central to your feelings of self-worth, or even focus on your partner's negative attributes, the relationship is infested with poison. It is essential to check within ourselves if we are constantly evaluating our relationships by someone else's rules and measurements. If the answer is yes, then it is time for a paradigm shift. Emotional intimacy is about shifting from evaluating each other to staying connected, to staying conscious and mindful about our relationship with each other.

CHAPTER 7

Enhancing Physical Intimacy

A key to any physical intimacy is how connected a couple is when they are not physically together. Connect spiritually with your own true nature, God, and through that channel connect deeply with each other (read previous chapter!). Focus during sexual encounters on what your partner needs but do not hesitate to communicate your own needs, too. Be present, aware, and compassionate to yourself (what really feels good and right for you) and to your partner. Cherish each other and not just each other's bodies! Cultivate a total approach in our life to the concept of the sacredness of sexual health in a combination of physical, emotional, mental, and spiritual energy. Maintain a sense of humor as an essential part of well-being.

Sharing sexual energy can be a most profound and powerful way to express deep love between partners when approached with awareness and care. Tantric teachings consider this aspect of relationship as sacred, likening sexual energy to life force, or kundalini energy, the very force behind creation itself. However, all too often this aspect of relationship is trivialized, compromised or fraught with confusion and ambivalence. In our view, it deserves a conscious approach, whether it takes on the style of Tantric ritual, loving spiritual communion or genuine selfish sweetness. There are principles that can take you towards your sexual nature responsibly, enhancing other aspects of your intimate life. Here are seven of them.

CHAPTER 8

Cultivating Mutual Respect

So, how might we practice the cultivation of mutual respect, love's essential partner, in our committed relationships? First, we deepen our careful attention in one another's unique inner and outer worlds, taking in what has meaning for our spouses. With this profound exchange, we ensure that each individual in the partnership is seen as truly significant. Once we've opened up this sensual connection, we can grow it further with deep listening, being available to hear others with our whole self. As we come to understand it, the institutions of marriage and family and the world function under certain courageous values. These values, passed on by our varied tribes or by our religious texts, differ little from religious teachings of common religions, including Buddhism. So regardless of creed, what is truly good – what is considered good universally – lays the foundation for basic relations that enhance the human experience.

The practice of mindfulness – paying attention in a kind and loving way – can help us become more conscious and conscientious partners. Conscientious love is about being open, considerate, heartfelt, and generous in intimate partnerships that last a lifetime. How do we begin to live and love this way? Cultivating mindful attributes that promote such love is a good place to start. The first article in this series focused on the theme of kindness. In this second follow-up article, we aim our attention at mutual respect. As human beings connected to all other living beings, we sense that every one of us is worthy of respect simply by virtue of being. But it is in our most intimate relationships that this respect is put to the test most of all. Here, we are greeted with our loved ones' physical, emotional, and spiritual needs as ones that can either generate trust or promote estrangement within our partnerships.

CHAPTER 9

Managing Conflict and Resolving Differences

Good marriages enhance the mental health of the partners. The incidences of depression, anxiety, paranoia, delusions, suicidality, hypochondriasis, substance abuse, sociopathy, and posttraumatic stress disorders: all are increased in people who are divorced or have never married when compared with people in long-term committed partnerships. Many of these problems are seen particularly in single parents and occur at twice the rate seen in two-parent families. Perhaps you have sometimes felt anxious since you began reading this section. Would recognizing that relationship difficulties are created by simple, common, universal transgressions make you feel a little less anxious as you think about the challenges in your own relationship? After all, there are ways of stepping successfully around all of these little divine mines and making sure that you do not step on any.

In every relationship, even the happiest and most compatible, partners see their lives differently and thus sometimes have differences of opinion that give rise to quarrels. Most couples have many disagreements each day. Yet only one in five married couples ever learns how to settle a quarrel in a way that brings satisfaction from both partners and promotes a deepening of the partnership as a result of the resolution. How to resolve the inevitable quarrel is the central underlying theme of The Mindful Marriage. That basic failure—to resolve conflicts in a satisfying way—lies buried beneath all the failed marriages that end in divorce. Conversely, it explains why a happy marriage makes both members of the partnership live longer, have better health, including fewer colds, and report a higher level of life satisfaction.

CHAPTER 10

Practicing Forgiveness and Letting Go

Always remember that in any marriage, it's not about who is right and who is wrong. It's not about who should say "I'm sorry." But whether the marriage is right for you! Marriage, my dear, isn't about carrying baggage. Any baggage. Weighing you down. Marriage isn't about one claiming the high ground. Or one weighing the pros and cons of leaving it all behind. Marriage isn't about who is stronger. Or who has the better sense of pride. Marriage isn't about who is strong or who can forgive. Marriage is about embracing the essence of love. Marriage is about filling your journey with light. Giving each other new reasons to live. Who are we to create reasons to break away?

In marriage, more often than not, we choose our partners from a fray of mismatched individuals. Two people from completely different perspectives in life, flung together to negotiate a joint journey. What is true for every other aspect of our lives is even truer in marriage. Personal biases, unresolved baggage from the past, and our faulty belief systems make it necessary to address conflicts very differently. Especially when they concern something that matters to both parties. If they didn't, then there would have been no conflict in the first place. It would be safe to say that most conflicts that arise in a relationship, whether acknowledged or not, are the outward manifestation of a deeper-seated need to affirm my individuality and self-worth – often at the expense of the other person. This essentially forms the basis of all misunderstandings and conflicts.

There is a Sufi story about a husband and wife who were constantly bickering over an issue that mattered to both of them. The silence that followed could only be described as a trench that could be cut with a knife. This went on for days, until the wife – a wise woman who knew a thing or two about what mattered – was forced by her husband to ask him a critical question, "I am angry, of course I am. But darling, why are you still angry?" As with all good Sufi stories, nothing more is said. The story is left to jolt the listener into provoking thought.

CHAPTER 11

Sustaining Love and Connection

The love was still there, and that was what they used as fuel to peg every throw and shot, every bump and rip, clear and dig. They were like two birds who soared gracefully and in tandem, ascending into illimitable realms—only they used their wings only for lunging forward and conveying their beloved ball across the abyss between hurt and joy. They usually stopped coming to see me when the crisis was over, after they navigated through opportunities to implement forgiveness and acceptance for the pain they caused each other. But last week, Maggie came in, telling me that she missed Jay. She missed Jay's friendship and random affection, the steadiness of his presence and the laughter they shared. She missed her strong and supportive partner in all things except conflict resolution and their continuing habit of misunderstanding and interrupting each other.

From the start of our work together, my clients Maggie and Jay have seen me individually as well as collectively. They usually come in as a couple, yet in the thick of a storm or toward the beginning of something huge. It helps to work with them both as a unit and as individual people. Besides enabling me to get to know each of them in their entirety, talking with them separately ensures that the cycle of bad habits and unhelpful communication is interrupted. It gives them the opportunity to say things and reveal long-hidden parts of themselves that they may find difficult to express in each other's presence. It allows me, with some direction, to restore dignity to the marriage and respect for each other.

CHAPTER 12

Creating Shared Meaning and Purpose

By definition, when you share your dreams and your plans with one another, there's a shared sense of meaning and purpose you can build upon concretely and tangibly. And there can never be enough discussion about actual talk around the meaning and purpose. This is the type of discussion that needs to last forever. Making sure that your life's work is not forgotten or put on hold is incredibly important. Make sure you find time to have these deep, important conversations, according to what you believe, what inspires you, and what you want to achieve. Never leave this groundwork in the back of your minds. Always discuss and keep that on the front burner. Don't forget your shared destiny and how it's so important.

What's your "house" built on, and on which solid ground does it stand? Houses that are built on sand may still be standing, but the foundation is weak, shifting, unsteady. There's no solid ground, no firm place to stand. Your marriage, modeled by the production of your "house" in this poem, is on the same tenuous ground if there isn't any purpose or meaning that keeps it steady. In fact, the notion of a "house" is a metaphor for just that. The intention behind discussion is to generate a house that's built on much more solid ground. When a couple talks about their dreams and goals and what they both would like to see together and be part of, they are essentially cultivating the foundation that their shared sense of meaning and purpose can stand on.

CHAPTER 13

Embracing Vulnerability and Authenticity

Remember this pivotal "I like you more and more, the clearer it becomes that you don't want to be here" scene in Good Will Hunting? It is a painful and resounding reminder of the countless times two people stand on the precipice of really connecting with one another only to recoil back into the safety of old patterns and belief systems. Our primitive need for belonging is thwarted by our fear of rejection or loss, so we hide our true selves and shield our hearts in a nearly impenetrable shroud of armor. But for every Good Will Hunting scene, there are a million more beautiful moments where we are loved for who we really are, where our hearts resonate because we were deeply seen, appreciated, and valued by another.

Brene Brown has revolutionized the way we think about human connection, vulnerability, and authenticity. Her TED talk "The Power of Vulnerability" has been viewed by millions – and for good reason. For many of us, connection is no longer even a consideration – it's an urgent hunger – yet our culture is scripting us to live as if we are separate, flawed, and unworthy. The antidote, Brown suggests, is a good dose of vulnerability and authenticity. It's easy to get psychologist-speak-y and say "We could all stand to be a little more vulnerable" or "Let's see a little authenticity here, people," as if being vulnerable or authentic is as simple as rolling up our sleeves and gritting our teeth. But it takes tremendous courage to be vulnerable or authentic when you are steeped in the conditioning of perfectionism in a society that values appearances and pretends, in most cases, to have it all figured out. But when we are willing to unravel our conditioning to cultivate these qualities, our relationships deepen in ways we could never imagine.

CHAPTER 14

Fostering Emotional Support and Empathy

Communication, empathy, respect, and support; used mindfully, these are the cornerstones of a healthy, successful OPI marriage. When the passion dims, work takes a toll, life's responsibilities take root, and leisure time becomes scarce, these elements are the glue that will keep couples together. When the passion reignites, passions are fulfilled, and dreams are realized, these same elements will bring married partners joy and spiritual fulfillment that will deepen their relationship forever.

It's important to note that to be able to fully engage in a mindful marriage, each member of the couple must feel that he or she can turn to the other for support and empathy. In her research, University of Washington marital expert, Dr. John Gottman found that early on in relationships, "emotional support" was the principal variable correlated with long term relationship success and satisfaction. More recently, Dr. Harry Reis, of the University of Rochester, found that when people are in a committed long-term relationship, they "typically perceive their partner to be an important source of support." As we mentioned in the chapter on Communication, Gottman's research also found that it is important to discuss problems with your partner and treat them with respect in order to receive the desired support because "if [you] made known to [the] partner that support was warranted, but the partner did not support that need, then the partner was not to be trusted."

Over the course of our lives, we all experience a broad range of challenges. Consciously choosing to be in a relationship with someone who cares deeply about you and is willing to support and empathize with you in good times and bad is a priceless gift. Whether it's a barb from a colleague, financial trouble, or a personal struggle, at times you may feel like you're up against the world all on your own. When you know there's someone in your corner who is dedicated to looking out for you, these challenges become much less overwhelming. With this kind of support lying the firm foundation of the relationship, partners are free to face life's challenges knowing that their relationship is the one thing in their lives that will steady and protect them.

CHAPTER 15

Balancing Independence and Togetherness

You are independent. You are together. Mutual freedom, I like to call it. For you to feel whole, enough, and free; and for you to stand beside and support another in their journey. A relationship is two people in it, together but not conjoined. Be enough. Enough for yourself. Fullulent in who you wish to become. Hand over the guiding reins. Recognize your dams or don't dams. Preferences. Insecurities. Let him construct his own space. Become a part of the space. Plan, dream, and envision alongside him. Both of your independent cells create an environment filled with respect and love. A complex vibrational network. Embraced. Influence. Executed.

In purposeful partnership, the sacred container that we both agreed to build becomes a mobile unit; the sides shift as we make decisions and explore uncharted territory. The entryway stays open in case you come back and sit with the space, take time to reflect, and then continue. It's flexible. Fluid. We can grow in it and will not become constrained.

As a couple, we brainstorm ideas, discuss how we can serve each other's endeavors, come up with a plan, and execute our decisions side by side. The other person doesn't rule the plan because you are both a part of the plan. I have learned that it is more important sometimes to take the risk, and it leads to inspiration. Inspiration leads to action and creates forward movement. It builds momentum and shows that you can paddle the canoe just as well as he/she can. You've got this. So be active. Inspire. Lead.

I used to fail horribly at independence because I would ask Henry for every detail about our plans, his plans, and our time together. It drove me crazy, and I'm sure that it drove him crazy. I didn't want to rock the boat and make the wrong decision in case I stepped on his toes. I have learned that it is healthier to make a mistake than to not make one at all.

For some of us, striking a balance is hard. This can be the case especially when we become a "we" and we lose ourselves a bit in the process. It's okay for a time, but if we make a practice of subsuming our individual needs, it leads to unhappiness, resentment, and anger. We matter. Our individual paths and happiness matter.

CHAPTER 16

Cultivating Gratitude and Appreciation

If you stay with Emmons's "gratitude challenge" for the suggested three weeks, your partner will most likely feel closer to you even if you tell him nothing about your practice, for the simple reason that it's impossible to practice gratitude without changing your patterns of thought. That person will generally feel surprisingly different, if only because it would be impossible not to pick up on the message that underlies your more appreciative tone or actions. In other words, Emmons's exercise will not make your partner love you more, but it will likely make him feel better about life and the relationship. And because his brain does a bit of emotional "copycatting," your partner will probably feel a tiny bit happier, just from the chemical changes associated with any shift toward a more positive state of mind.

The structure of your brain makes it all too easy to take people for granted. When something or someone is always there, you stop noticing what that person means to you, or how much of a difference that person's presence makes. If your partner acts respectfully, you start expecting respectful behavior - and then tend to notice only when your partner fails to act that way. That's why psychologist Robert Emmons suggests that we set ourselves a daily gratitude challenge. Emmons, one of the world's experts on the cultivation of gratitude, says that regular expression of appreciation for others helps us focus on what we value - and what we don't, but should. This process leaves us feeling happier and more satisfied with our relationships, even if the one we address has no idea we think this way. The opposite also holds: Expressions of love deepen our own appreciation of the person we love.

CHAPTER 17

Strengthening Friendship and Companionship

While many would deem trust vital for marriages to succeed, it could be argued it is essential for a successful marriage. Trust is the foundation on which all relationships are built. It is vital in all relationships whether romantic, social or professional, and once lost, it is one of the most challenging things to rebuild. When all the aspects of marriage are stripped down, it is revealed a happy and lasting union is tied together with threads of respect for one another. Respect involves helping one's partner to become the best version of themselves. It encompasses elements such as mutual respect and admiration and it may also mean empowering, validating, and valuing one another. Couples in mindful marriage integrate the thread of respect into the other aspects of their marriage to ensure their relationship blooms and time brings them even closer.

Marriage is comprised of many aspects that together form the foundation of a strong relationship. Marriage is about connecting on a more intimate level, and that level involves friendship and companionship. Regardless of how long a couple has been together, one person should always be able to talk easily and laugh with the other. Friendship could be about honesty, trust, being truthful to one another, or being emotionally supportive. Friendship involves both parties to create a balance between reaching out to one another without feeling overwhelmed or burdened. The happy couples who let us into the secret of their long-term relationships can teach us that growing old gracefully together boils down to giving equal measure to passion and real friendship, or companionship if you will.

CHAPTER 18

Navigating Life Transitions Together

Marriage, at its hopeful best, is enlightenment at work, living in actual conditions and under totally unfair terms, a journey which two exuberantly radiant souls in an unpalatable human form undertake as they bleed and cry and, then, smile, and learn—and, finally, laugh at the futility and farcicalness of the journey—and then laugh with the tears of joy and consummation on their cheeks. That laughter and freedom brings a universe inside a relationship to life—are you and your partner nurturing such a thing?

If we could extend that symbol into the years and decades of marriage that follow? We can, and it's a never-ending—and astonishingly beautiful—experiment in our development, learning to coalesce the unique powers and capabilities and inclinations of a unique individual with those of another to serve the larger good of the true entity that a positive and mindful marriage is.

One of the greatest modernized wedding traditions that I love is the unity candle. It's simple, profound, and clear: one candle represents the life and experiences and existence of one person, and another the other person, and they merge together to fulfill the rest of their days! It's beautiful in its symbolisms, and the merging into one flame has a mesmerizing visual aspect that always captivates the mind's eye.

CHAPTER 19

Mindful Parenting in a Conscious Marriage

It is stating the obvious that raising children together demands a good connection between parents. The emotional and communication skills that characterize a conscious parental relationship are the same skills that are formed upon the same teachings that underlie a conscious marriage. The family "is an integral part of the transformation that serves as a training ground to grow your awakened self" and parents who make life enriching changes in their commitment may be seen as role models for the development of their children who can similarly "develop the necessary skills that deepen the spiritual, emotional, and psychological roots important for an awakening interconnected chronic world." A conscious marriage, in simple terms, consists of a sacred commitment and willingness of partners to be present, pay attention to, open to and accept each other, as well as those relationships that shape their experience of family, career, and various communities.

Once this trust is built, couples can consider how the principles of conscious parenting can be applied to help them deepen connection to the very core of their partnership and cultivate a more mindful and profound union. But what exactly does the phrase conscious marriage mean? This seems just as much an oxymoron as conscious parenting is, as it denotes a commitment to being fully aware and present with each other, embracing vulnerability, and building deep and mindful connection through contemplative dialogue and practice. The principles of conscious parenting are necessary to enhance the energy, focus, responsibility, and attention that drives not only the mindful marriages but also other types of relationships including the ones in therapy. According to Eckhart Tolle, in fact, it is by encountering the conflict that graps may help us raise what would have been a "soul mate" relationships to a more profound conscious love relationship or marriage, for the greater level of conflict in the soul mate relationship encourages more consciousness.

CHAPTER 20

Prioritizing Self-Care and Personal Growth

We suggest that self-expansion theory lies at the heart of mindfulness practice. Indeed, mindful individuals truly expand their lives in many areas, which require the "presencing" of their own thoughts and actions, and they approach conflict mindfully. As individuals become more adept at living mindfully, they are equipped to expand on and deepen their selves in a number of different domains. Throughout life, our partners help us grow as individuals by introducing us to new people and activities. When we live consciously, we encourage our spouse to experiment with a wider range of experiences and co-construct lifestyles that can accommodate the growth of both partners. Using mindfulness to connect to and expand the self, couples improve their relationships - intimidating, as self-expansion researchers suggest, couples can enjoy "marital longevity".

While the notion of prioritizing personal growth seems, to many, synonymous with becoming the best possible human beings we can be, it is actually instrumental to a conscious marriage as well. In fact, personal growth is simultaneously a cause and a product of stable, enduring marriages. Linking the individual to the individual partner, the individual partner to the partnership, and the partnership to the outside world, marital satisfaction and longevity improve when partners seek to learn and grow through marriage. Self-expansion theory purports that couples can come to appreciate and "love" one another more if their partnership causes each person to become more than they might have become alone. Furthermore, personal growth continuously energizes and renews a couple's connection to each other, and increases and perpetuates marital satisfaction over the life of the partnership.

CHAPTER 21

Maintaining Work-Life Balance

The characteristics of balance differ from person to person, but most agree it is possible. This concept is echoed in a Special Report: Work/Life Balance provided by the presenter. Together, with those working in large and small businesses, government entities, and those that are self-employed in the private sector, we uncover common strategies for keeping balance in a world full of priorities, opportunities, and challenges. Other commonalities with these lists address the importance of scheduling time for relaxation. Although specifics differ, educators primarily suggest leaving work behind, where independent professionals and parents/dual-career professionals comment on a passion and budget required to maintain success in the home and at work. Lastly, there is an agreement regarding the importance of practice and reflection. As we identify more segments of inspiration from gender to working conditions, these lists direct our outlook and process, ensuring an opportunity to grow and grow balanced relationships.

The assignment was simple: compile a list of tips and advice for living a balanced life, particularly for parents in a modern, achievement-oriented, or career-focused situation. The answers to the question "What can we do to achieve and maintain work-life balance?" were insightful, and this concept was echoed among respondents. Jenni Harris, the mother of 4 and owner/senior broker at Windermere Realty/Jenni Harris & Associates, stated, "Next year I'll be celebrating 20 years in the real estate industry. Throughout that time, I have worked in 4 different firms, and my business has thrived in spite of the real estate crash in 2008. In other words, I am grateful for work and the flexibility associated with self-employment. Early on in my career, I had to repeatedly tell clients 'I cannot meet with you at 10 am.' My situation is unique, but there are a few concepts that are relevant regardless of profession. The following are my tips for maintaining work/life balance as an independent professional and as a parent."

CHAPTER 22

Building a Supportive Network

The process of connecting with a partner's world guides couples in creating and maintaining essential friendships that provide support, wisdom, and laughter. Shared associations provide group approval for couples' plans and commitments, which can lead to an enriching environment. Factors for well-being, ranging from friendship to problem-solving, have been shown to correlate with marital happiness. Shared connections enable a couple to feel validated and to gather different perspectives to understand and cope with life's challenges, and support many another couple dare to attempt tasks which they could not manage single-handedly. Because the world of each spouse may be necessary to complete agreements with friends, proximity of the friendship is among the highest indications of pleasing former or later stages of marriage. Close relationships, defined as shared positive activities, are at the surface shared by pleasant youths and the grown-ups. Associations act in a similar way to family interactions, constructing strategies and prospects which stand-by for all. Each day, one takes time for comfort, envy, and pride in his friendship. Realizing that one truly is comfortable, blessed, and proud of the most faithful partnership produces a well-being which is sustainable.

One key aspect of a mindful marriage involves broadening the sense of "we" rather than "me" and building a supportive network of friends and family. As one of us used to tell students in his Positive Psychology course, "Surveys ask: 'Who do you live with?' They don't ask, 'Who do you live for?' But research on well-being consistently shows that the latter matters much more - whom we live for, or love. Or as C.S. Lewis explains it, "The people who keep their lives will lose them; and the people who give up their lives will find them."

CHAPTER 23

Exploring Shared Interests and Hobbies

Although some may view this as indigent and believe they should obtain validation through success and stature via traditional social competition, living within the means that society dictates to us is no way to live a life, but rather an existence. In the end, it is the duty of every individual traversing the spiritual path to wake up, smell the coffee-kind in the air, completely engulfed by the taste and aroma of intoxicating union, and love compassionately being awake.

Shared hobbies can strengthen bonds, all the while offering individuals an intricate look into their partners' world. They can also help to rebuild an identity that was lost due to prolonged isolation in phases of one's life thus far. Participating in these new hobbies becomes a means of obtaining validation and satisfaction, yet is unencumbered by social competition. It is the activity itself and the personal fulfillment obtained from the act that provides self-assurance and not the act of competition.

Individuation, however, does not have to come through comparative rivalry, nor does it have to be competitive. It can instead come from exploring shared interests, embarking on new hobbies and endeavors that have the potential for positive introspection and mutual personal and spiritual growth.

Individuation can be accomplished through various means, including social competitiveness. When the acquisition of material goods has run its course and could no longer hold the same appeal it used to provide, due to owning more things than one can possibly have a use for, those same individuals who sought footing and validation via the act of impressing others with their material wealth often find themselves adrift, having lost parts of their identity and sense of self that were in part formed from the activity.

CHAPTER 24

Cultivating a Sense of Adventure and Fun

Intimacy peaks between partners don't usually last forever. Ex-psychologists John Gottman, MD, and Julie Campbell, MD, believe that successful couples master the art of nurturing regular connections which result in both emotional and spiritual intimacy. They suggest that no matter what type of personal constitution and inclination you hold or how greatly you are connected to another, it's important to also build in time for fun because a relationship generally thrives on joyousness. Gottman and Campbell recommend taking the time to jointly participate in novel, out-of-the-ordinary experiences without a pre-established agenda. Try to make your partner laugh every day. Dr. Ilene Cristinand Michael Cristini, visiting Professor of Philosophy at Salve Regina University, suggest that intimate relationships prosper much more when love is expressed humorously and through a good, lively sharing of fun.

As you can probably surmise, choosing the sacred path of marriage can lead to major growth opportunities and a serious adventure—or put another way, a roller-coaster ride. By opening to a conscious relationship, we are invited to cultivate more passion, friendship, love, understanding, honesty, flexibility, playfulness, expansion, gratitude, and generosity—with ourselves and others, including animals and the

Earth. True, the path of a relationship isn't always a bed of roses or a walk in the park. In order to experience the love and joy that is possible, you have to be willing to move through the many layers that make up the onion of your psyche, be gutsy enough to share your emotions and intimate thoughts, keep the Mystery and a good sense of humor alive, and cultivate a genuine willingness to grow.

CHAPTER 25

Practicing Mindfulness in Everyday Life

To cultivate mindfulness in everyday life, one should ensure that no systemic precondition singles them out. Extending to the observer involved, intentions and interrelations can provoke unwanted conditioning. Examples include gratification by naming, delight by hailing, disappointment by default, confusion by more of the same, despair by design. In stark contrast, covening experienced as consumer units (points of vacuum) make the world persist to our mind and evaporate into utter oblivion. Compassion and peace flourish in relationship, communication, limits, individuality, prudence, creativity, evaluation, bias, utilization, objects, action, respect, reciprocity, depersonalization, transcendence. This relationship, however, is not subjected to general natural patterns of relative predictability and inherent variability. Therefore, genuine reliance on relationship as an improved way does not flow. Mutual encouragement is difficult to divine—or chooses to someone—when it fits a conclusive explanation for meaningless severe failures or massive changes. Considering mutual encouragement, how much meaningful information is needed to either enable or disable impairment functionality through prejudice, stereotype, discrimination, segregation?

The more we practice mindfulness in everyday life, the more we inspire and are inspired by goodness and peace instead of by dehumanizing reasons such as crude social mock-ups and dumb revulsion. While awareness of what is happening in the here and now is essential, our main challenge would then be to hold the tension of life right-handedly. People may have the conventional aim of minimizing inner noise, but statistical shortcuts are rife with variations of dependency and disregard that it should not happen way too often. This answer is conditionally arguably difficult and often evaded. The practice of mindfulness causes severe difficulties for seven days a week, not to the cat in the woods but to the kittens in the laboratory or to someone in the middle of time-less endless activity. In a similar way, mindfulness unmotivates us to label others as bad, problematic or ugly. Really listening with a strong intention to focus does not lead to the predominance of external, time-consuming judgmental sectionals. Consequently, when someone acts interested as a spiritual or cultural observance, there is commonly no sufficiently strong ethical intuition; there is still some other pretext that promotes the postponement of peace and love for specifics such as earnest agreements and pointless anxieties.

CHAPTER 26

Deepening Spiritual Connection

27. Honor Intimacy in Your Relationship Intimacy is a sweet smelling rose; the more you cultivate it, the more it blossoms. The success of any relationship is largely dependent on the level of intimacy that exists between two partners. Keep in mind that at the very center of each of us resides our vibrant and beautiful soul. It uses the body as a living vehicle to enhance its interactions and experiences. Covering up the spiritual essence of any individual is like trying to conceal the sun with your fingers; it will never yield a satisfactory result for you. Your partner has the sacred responsibility of encouraging and helping you to live and express your soul more fully. When you honor the spiritual essence of your partner, you have already provided him or her with the most precious gift. You have unspokenly conveyed the message that you acknowledge and adore the resident temple of yourself. Always honor this gift by treasuring it if you wish to watch it grow. When you appreciate the spiritual side of your partner, the acknowledgment sweetens your intimacy further, thus opening up the pathway to deeper realms of love and also bounds of closeness you never dreamt or imagined it was possible to experience.

The overall potential of your relationship is not limited to what you can see with the naked eye. Focusing on how your partner looks, what he or she does for a living, and what he or she has achieved so far dampens the true potentials you can realize via the gateway of your spiritual connection. Every difficulty or obstacle you encounter in your relationship has the capacity to launch you into higher consciousness. Accept and honor them, celebrating the fact that they are here to re-direct your attention to something that has been overlooked. Whenever couples experience a difficult patch in their relationship, they are forced to look within and redefine what the relationship is really about. Always remember that any disconnection between the two of you is actually the sagging of the connection, due to the weight of your unconsciousness.

CHAPTER 27

Overcoming Relationship Challenges

When effort is made and trust is maintained, love is refueled as a new cycle is made. Very few things can weaken a relationship if partners become honest communicators and committed to undertaking various facets that require daily nurturing. You could take a minute every day to evaluate your bond, appreciate your partner, and learn from mistakes. Be responsible, and you will be amazed by how simple things become. Becoming responsible, acknowledging who you are, and appreciating your contributions ensures you are invaluable in every tryst. It's the contribution that counts. Sometimes people realize their actual composition in life and assume responsibilities that have already been made important. Be appreciative, and you will have the assurance that you are important simply as you are.

The following are some of the challenging and often insidious relationship dilemmas that can unravel even the most loving marriages: high level of discord, ongoing financial problems, preventing infidelity, in-law problems, emotional unavailability, trust issues, fights, and repetitive arguments, life balance and unmatched approaches, trying to get past bad history, being a rebuilder. If you appreciate the fact that long-term relationships require commitment and respect from both partners, you realize that relationships need constant nurturing. That way, it is truly possible to grow old with expectations of new stories happening; similarly, the stories that thrill, stories that hurt, stories that make you feel great, as well as the stories that foster positive growth.

CHAPTER 28

Seeking Professional Help and Guidance

The marriage, in some rare, uniquely and truly suffering instances, might admit temporary recess through a conscious loving, seeking deep guidance. As indicated many times over, this is in no way the simple option (however it may appear to be the easier way out) that conscientious individuals might choose when they are overwhelmed by the intensity of the moment and the certainty that they really no longer want to continue their suffering. Through consciousness, additional suffering is deliberately being assumed. Nevertheless, enduring, healing, and forgiving through deep acknowledging are truly the supreme challenges we confront in couplehood or being on our solitary path. More often than not, Love and Nature seem to almost conspire, repeatedly providing pathways through marriage pain (i.e. forgiveness and healing) from ways that are least suspected but which, in the long run, are in many not necessarily embarked on in seeking the ephemeral and destructive protections of the conventional hasty and angry truths.

It can become really difficult for a couple, as it had become for Annie and Jack, to bridge the gap that develops when they seem so far apart from each other. And when the emotional intensity is at its highest, when the risk of infidelity is greatest, and when one or both individuals simply might not have the capacity to hold and honor the intensity of their suffering relationship, the temptation to put an end to the intense suffering is too great. It's here that professional help is crucial. It helps a couple by providing an external container to gently hold the totality of their relationship, supporting the partners (individually and as a couple) by nurturing and providing the necessary guidance, inspiration, and hope to move forward. It might also help them accept that the end of the conventional forms of connection and parentage might have to be done. Not temporarily or in any way lightly conceived. Not based on anger, disappointment, or frustration. But — almost unspeakable for many and seemingly an improbable outcome — out of love and with respect.

Fostering Resilience and Adaptability

To the degree that Ari and Jennifer's story sounds familiar, it is important to continuously ask: in what would have been the real in that present moment? Certainly the belief in thoughtless living shows us that much busyness we waste ourselves in provides no meaningful value, and that much tendency to care deeply about unimportant things suffocates our growth as conscious beings. When influenced to act to please others or to please ourselves, we can begin to ask - what purpose does our action hold? What degree of individual will does our activity require? Start being mindful. Start right here and now - when examining human capacities, when identifying impediments to flow. Deny abstract constructs based on arbitrary moral ideas or the transgressions of your past. How can the development of your lives be reciprocal?

The trouble was, Ari and Jennifer led busy lives. Their awareness was monopolized by machines - emails, cell phones, deadlines, classes to prepare, clients to satiate. It seemed impossible to devote more time to "us" and to the space it would require, a most basic impossibility at the core of the nearest of intimacies. Focusing on his family was especially challenging for Ari, as he had grown up in a household characterized by frequent emotional and physical outbursts. Although Jennifer knew in intellectual ways that making time for their emotional bond was important, she forgot just how important it actually was and what it felt like to come alive and open - resilient and adaptive - with Ari after difficult times pushed her toward silence, anger, or rigidity.

CHAPTER 30

Celebrating Milestones and Achievements

Research has also shown that couples who celebrate frequently are more likely to feel motivated, try new things, work towards each other's goals, and avoid division caused by lack of awareness and effort. If celebration is added to physical intimacy and emotional friendship, a couple will develop an ever-strengthening union. And therein lies the revelation that I struggled to accept: the health of advanced stages (later stages) of romantic relationships relies on the continued work that helped build the earlier stages. Just as physical intimacy needs to be maintained, and emotional friendship continuously strengthened, nurtured friendship needs to be cared for. When this is met with like mindfulness, a couple celebrates a never-ending bounty.

How do you celebrate milestones and achievements in your relationship? Whether couples choose small, yet meaningful gestures, have regular designated celebrations, or use rare and significant accomplishments as excuses for lavish parties, it is critical that they make time and show appreciation for the hard work and dedication that leads to a successful achievement. In fact, celebrated psychologist John Gottman determined that couples are more likely to stay together if they maintain a minimum preponderance of positive emotions and experiences relative to negative ones. That less than perfect relationships will develop disconnection and unhealthy dynamics is a given. It is essential that couples set time aside to be present and focused on their mate during accomplishments, so that they don't take their positioning for granted (a deserving entity of resentment instead).

CHAPTER 31

Reflecting on the Journey Together

Looking back at their life journey involves celebrating their love journey, while recognizing that the journey isn't all about love. It isn't about transcendent, ever satisfying rapture. Love's journey is not always rewarding nor enjoyable, and one's "everlasting love" journey, described through love maps and love narratives, is not exempt from life's more mundane stressors. Partners manage the practical bulk of planning, surviving, and recovering from great life challenges, including recovering from great loss, giving birth or aiding with the birth of a child, supporting one another after a diagnosis of illness, addressing concerns related to personal notions of death and dying and providing practical support posthumously. Mindful couples appreciate that such topics as the end of life are not morbid or disturbing to consider. Mindful couples see exploring mutual values, considerations, and concerns related to end of life enjoyable, nourishing activities of love that can emotionally and logically bring them back to talking about family, friends, joy and the value of personal love, or appreciating the great moments of a past end of life passage in their life.

The challenge for many committed partners is to navigate life's journey with mindful awareness. The joy of the early phase of a romantic relationship is an experience of being "in the moment," experiencing now without judgment. Two people who agree to commit to one another do so from a mindful place, reflecting on their personal journey and celebrating the discovery of their unique partner. The newly betrothed can joyfully reflect on the past with their partner, open to the excitement of being a co-creator of the future. Mindful reflection can fortify such a relationship as it travels through the stages of love: limerence, passion, engagement, marriage, honeymoon, disappointment, distance, connection, celebration, challenge, and re-engagement. Wise co-journaling—sharing private journals, engaging in couple-focused reflection activities—can deepen the mindfulness for the journey. To continue to be in the moment in the face of challenge is a conscious act of love. There are some who would argue that passion never grows in relationships. From a mindful framework, however, authentic passionate connection is developed. Passion is a highly mindful act, with participants continually creating, sharing, and celebrating one another. To attend fully to a partner's life journey allows for omnipresent dedication to emotional connection.

CHAPTER 32

Conclusion

Couples are the foundation for building an embroidered tapestry of life. With every intention and act—each triumph, lesson, and blip along the journey—you're manifesting a pair of dedicated souls pledged to bringing love, light, understanding, and peace to each individual, and to your relationship's purpose and the splendid world supporting your efforts. Breathe into the energy now swirling about you. Absorb the power of divine love and blessings sent from the mystical, wondrous light that lives within you and through all the spirit-rich heavens. Great wisdom is being unveiled. Yield to its fierce energy and tamper not its fiery glow. Lift your faces and feel the warmth of ethereal resonance as it gently coaxes your lips into a knowing smile. Quietly thank the source for its serene, illuminating grace. And when the time comes, honor and unleash the magnificence of your heart's divinely designated treasures. You are now preparing to co-create a mindful marriage.

In addition to the exploration of the many facets of a conscious union, we have supplied numerous opportunities to attend to your relationship and invite Spirit's guidance. Your journey into The Mindful Marriage and toward a conscious relationship with your beloved is a highly personal quest. By setting aside the time to complete the soul-provoking exercises and meditations we've offered, you'll be better prepared for the rough spots, more fully experience the glorious connection

—soul-to-soul, heart-to-heart, and body-to-body—of your union, and delve into the deep spiritual purpose woven into your relationship.